THE LEGEND OF THE ISLE
by
R. A. PARSONS

THE LEGEND
OF THE ISLE

BY

R. A. PARSONS

Published by
THE ONTARIO PUBLISHING COMPANY LIMITED
DON MILLS, ONTARIO

Printed and bound in Canada
T. H. Best Printing Company Limited

Dedication

To the memory of Reverend Henry Gordon, Itinerant Missionary to Labrador 1915-1925 and John Lewis Paton, M.A., 1st President of Memorial University College.

Acknowledgment

The author wishes to thank Miss Eleanor Whittle, for the assistance given him in the preparation of this volume.

Frontispiece by Reginald Shepherd

Foreword

G. A. FRECKER, O.C., B.A., B.E., LL.D.

We should all be the poorer were it not for men like Mr. R. A. Parsons, Q.C., the author of this little volume. He is among those who not only share our love of this rugged, buffetted, but beautiful and picturesque historic land and its warm-hearted people, but who in addition experience a strong urge to express and record their observations, their experiences, their feelings, with keen sensitivity.

In so doing, our artists, chroniclers and poets ensure that ways of life which gave Newfoundland its essence of being will not be completely obliterated by the hammer blows of the irresistible changing conditions of modern times.

All too frequently writers on Newfoundland have tended to concentrate on the less pleasant, harsher aspects of its history and life. Undoubtedly, hardship, adversity and even tragedy have been much in evidence down the years, but that is not the whole story, or Newfoundland would not have such a hold on its people.

For those of us no longer counted young it is a source of pleasure to read in quiet moments the sympathetic and evocative word paintings of a Newfoundland way of life well known to us but fast passing from view.

In years to come, Newfoundlanders will read Mr. Parson's nostalgic reminiscences and be enriched by a better understanding of days which have gone with the winds of material progress, but which nevertheless gave Newfoundland its distinctiveness, its character and its charm.

Thank you, R.A. for your labour of love. We are the richer for your several books — and the present little work in which inter alia you unravel the mystery of Kelly's Island; describe life in the tiny fishing settlement of Fair Haven; commune with the sprightly little sparrow on a cold, frosty morning, and share with us your meditations in the beautiful Anglican Cathedral of St. John the Baptist.

G. A. Frecker.

Contents

My verse is of our Island that the sea
Hath so indented or so fashioned, we
As creatures seeming of the self same tide
Along its bays and fiords, so formed, reside;
And so if I am, as perchance you'll find,
To ships and sailormen too much inclined,
Or prone to favour these beyond their meed,
My home, thus fashioned, for my fault must plead.

The Legend of the Isle

Somewhere along the line of his forebears
'Tis not unlikely there were buccaneers
Or roist'ring pirates, for he often told
Of dark adventure and ill-gotten gold;
Howe'er, I do not think that he would fight
Unless against injustice and of right,
Nor would he lend his succor or support
To any cause, unless convinced he ought;
But then again, grave wrongs unfairly borne
Tempt honest men, laws made by man, to scorn —
To do what they in time might sadly rue,
Should they too brash their remedies pursue —
And causes all have virtues, and no few
Have vices too, unknown until review,
As witnesseth the tale of those who've died
The dubious cause of princes to decide.

If some old sire of his had told that he
Had sailed their retributive in piracy,
We might explain just why my friend delights
In black-hulled rakish ships and running fights

Or why perchance his scion revels in
The tales of rogues and such who sail in sin.

His hair had finished whit'ning, but it spread
In billowing snow about his rev'rend head.
His eyes were brown and mischievous, but he
Employed them, and no doubt effectively,
To emphasize a risk or danger grave
Or his brave tales, from disbelief to save.
His face was lean, salt-toughened, bronzed, for he
Had spent most of his fourscore years at sea —
Signed on, not careful of the route or way,
Through Polar wastes, or seas that wash Cathay.
I judged him six feet tall; but stooping he
By habit bore himself deceptively.

He loved to yarn, and this I think was why
He favoured me, for hungrily would I
Upon him and his narrative await
Which he from time to time would punctuate
With puffs of smoke that issued from a pipe
Well seasoned, and I thought, a trifle ripe.
It seemed at times he wished to aggravate
Or test my patience, or perchance abate
My interest; but I can truly state
He never changed his leisured even gait.
And thus without a sign or trace of guile
In solemn tones he told me of an isle

That lay about a league from our shore
Of which I thought I knew as much or more
Than he, familiar as it was to me;
But he invested it with mystery.

Through summer months we boys occasion'ly
Would go there bound upon discovery.
By dinghy, dory, skiff or some such boat,
We'd row to it; but scant was there to note
Upon the isle, save now and then a goat,
A sheep or two, let loose through summer days
Upon wild grass abundant there to graze;
Yet notwithstanding all of this, he told
Of treasure there in coin and bars of gold
And I believed his story for you see
He told it to me so convincingly.

Upon this isle, he said, arose three mounds
Raised long ago whereof he knew no bounds:
Two marked the graves he said of two men slain
The secret of the third mound to maintain
Of treasure hid, a ghoul alone might claim,
Beneath it, laid between the murdered twain.
He dropped the matter then, and for a while
He would not, or it seemed, discuss the isle,
And spoke of inlets round Conception Bay
That likely could provide a hideaway
For vessels suspect of unlawful trade

Enabling these, the Kings ships to evade;
Then dealt with rogues reputed to have been
About our waters which he took to mean
Our bay; then as with it again concerned
He to the subject of the isle returned —

No other graves are there. These three alone
Are all that can be seen or have been known
Upon the isle, and from an early day
Or since folks settled round Conception Bay
They have in all their villages, he said,
With proper Christian rites interred their dead,
And none would be so lost to love, so vile,
As to inter a corpse on Kelly's Isle.
And thus the mounds, to no one's vast surprise,
Caused questioning, and many to surmise
That some lone ship off course and in our seas
Of fever smitten, or of some disease
Obscure contagious, out of mortal fear,
Had buried those who perished of it there;
But there were some who other causes gave
Accounting for the presence of each grave;
But I, he said, by his strange tale would see
How truth could counter probability
To such degree that not a man was found
To enter or explore the middle mound,
Until the facts about it had been learned
The facts with which his tale would be concerned,

And then from facts or his invention, he
Regaled me with the treasure's history:

Adverting now and then to Morgan or
To Eason, rogues familiar with our shore,
He introduced me to the way of life
The customs, habits, conduct and the strife
Of buccaneers;
Informed me of their ships, that they unseen
In inlets deep would these careen and clean
For only vessels furbished, lissome, sleek,
Might from pursuing frigates distance keep
Beyond their cannon range, or these elude
Until to follow further they'd no mood;
Of how they would in coves like ours procure
Fresh water, firewood and take and cure
The flesh of beasts and fish, could pick and store
In case of scurvey, berries wild galore;
Of how the crews from shipboard-watch released
Might do, in places such, as they so pleased.

Such men, he said, took discipline from none
But him of ready blade and deadly gun
And of such navigating skill that he
Became their chief of their necessity.

He paused awhile, then said he could not see
How sailors could remain in piracy —

I find, he said, that those who ply the sea,
Are prone in time to learn humility,
For they are constant minded as they sail
Across the trackless wastes how they must fail
Should heaven above deprive them of resource
In sun or star to plot their daily course.
True seamen sense a sympathy profound
Between the firmament and them abound —
And cannot viewing such benevolence
Remain insensible to Providence!

Of such an one he spoke at length, for he
Would 'stablish him, he said, in infamy
For when this scamp had duelled with and slain
The husband, that he might his widow gain
But to his chagrin, found his effort vain
To earn in place of favour her disdain,
He'd stol'n the lady's son and vengefully
Had borne the lad he'd orphaned off to sea
Upon a ship engaged, or thought to be
In contraband or outright piracy.

Now strange to say this man affection knew
And steadily toward the child he drew
For as the days went by, upon him grew
A fondness for the lad whose sire he slew —
From that attraction which it seems a child
Can oft exert upon a creature wild —

And he from time to time in kindness turned
Toward the boy; but he seemed unconcerned
For in him still no doubt resentment burned
Toward the man, and his affection spurned.
Thus for a while his ways expressed his mood;
Howe'er in time, less hostile or more shrewd
The boy became less prone to sulk or brood
Upon his wrongs, and changed his attitude
Until it seemed he had his wrongs forgot
Or he had grown contented with his lot.

The master ruled his ship, and every hand
Obeyed his word or gesture of command.
Her crew drawn from a pool of human scum
Of cutthroats, thieves and rascals on the run
In utter need of refuge turned to him
And succor found, withal his discipline,
And disobedience to his law they knew
Swift execution of harsh sanctions drew.
The boy found life aboard the vessel hard
Where ev'ry man on her was a blackguard
But by command they might not well neglect
The Captain saved him from their disrespect,
And as at variance with his nature he
Protected him from their brutality,
And woe be tide the man who'd hurt the boy
Or would in anyway the lad annoy.

And for the most part he was left alone
In freedom absolute the ship to roam
And subject to but prohibitions few
Was well nigh free to do what he might do;
Nor was he at the threat'ning of a gale
Allowed aloft in helping take in sail.
And at the sign of an encounter, he
Looked constant to the boy's security;
And as he wished no doubt the boy to be
Of rank above the common seaman, he
Taught him to read and write and calculate.
As master to apprentice should relate
He taught the boy as well to navigate.
A strange man thus so contradictory —
Who might determine his philosophy!
Thus was it with him till the years between
His capture and release had stretched thirteen:
Release that offered when the vessel lay
Within the waters of Conception Bay!
Off Kelligrews and close upon a mile
Due South or thereabouts from Kelly's Isle.

The ship had coursed in here 'twas understood
To take on water fresh and firewood
And two boats had been lowered to abide
Their uses for the purposes implied;
But unaccountably were left to ride:
One at the port, the other starboard side

(At this my friend told me that he preferred
I hear the story as it should be heard —
As from the boy's own lips and thus did he
Take up again the treasure's history).

The crew might ponder on this odd delay
But not a word would they attempt to say
Too mindful, fearful of his wrath that he
Might vent upon their curiosity.
With this delay, I was not too concerned
Till strange to say, the Captain to me turned
And beckoned me to come with him below
Into his spacious cabin to bestow
On me a packet bound secure, and sealed
Not to be opened or contents revealed
Until his death. And with the packet he
In cryptic utterance spoke thus to me
    "I am about to do what I have purposed long
      That I to some degree may right a wrong.
      I dare not wait or this thing more delay
      What I propose to do, I do today
      For who can tell where on the seas so wide
      The King's ships cruise, where now the frigates
          ride?
      It may be at this very moment they
      Decide to enter and to search this Bay!
      And should they unembarrassed by the night
      Discover us without recourse in flight

What then — although outmatched we must defy
And as condemned already, fighting die.
(How strange was it, that I so soon could note
How like a seer, a prophet, then he spoke)
"It is so with you, he said, your years
Will plead your pardon, you need have no fears.
This packet that is yours, I trust will tend
The evil I have done you to amend."
But as discovered in some act, that he
Would none on earth or heaven to see,
He changed; and as unto himself restored,
In real or simulated wrath he roared
At me, and naming then of rogues a pair
He bade me fetch them to his cabin, where
He wished, as I supposed, to interview
Them both beyond the hearing of the crew.

I was familiar with the cabin and the gear
He chose to let me see and overt there;
But ere I left to fetch the rogues, I saw
A great sea-chest I had not seen before —
Exposed but late to view I thought — but I
Would not have long to wait to learn just why,
For soon, I saw that very chest again
Borne to the deck and by his trusty twain,
Then lowered by them cautiously and slow
Into the boat that starboard lay below,
The Captain standing by: and furthermore

Aboard the boat the same two men I saw
The Captain too at steering, as she bore
Towards the isle, then round its Northern Shore,
Then west, as I surmised, and out of view
Beyond the vision of the vessel's crew.

Oh, I have asked myself again, again
Why I, despite the risk, decided then
To journey to the isle; but this I did
And when the boat was from the vessel hid,
I snatched the dinghy and in haste shot forth
Toward the isle, upon a course due North!
Thus I had clambered up the isle before
Their boat had beached upon its Northern Shore
And found a spot wherefrom with little fear
I, unobserved by them, could see and hear.

I heard them ask, and ere they had begun:
Why make three holes when there's but need of one,
And his reply: "You make them to deceive
All who chance by and lead them to believe
That these be graves of seamen, who have died
Of fever, likely buried side by side."
I heard them laugh upon his ready wit
And watched them work till they had leave to quit
And take a drink, a gen'rous draft of rum
The last for both, for as they drank, his gun
Spat twice —

Both staggered, tried, it seemed, themselves to save
But fell, each in his open ready grave!
Of horror stricken at that dreadful sight
I could not move, my limbs rejected flight
A dizziness, a faintness on me lay
But at recovery, I ran away.
I did not for a moment pause, remain
To see him cover in the men he'd slain,
Or hide the treasure laid between the twain;
And as I ran, as by the murdered men
Urged on, I vowed and vowed again, again
Of my abhorrence of this deed so vile
That were I left to perish on this isle
In consequence of my resolve to stay,
I never would rejoin the ship that lay
Awaiting him; and passing strange to say
In need of succor then, I learned to pray!

By heaven or by instinct moved, I found
A place to hide on elevated ground
With brush well covered, where I found I could
Observe the Captain when and as he would
Proceed toward the strand and boat, when he
Had finished with his task of infamy —
And scant time passed when it was manifest
That he would do indeed what I had guessed
And unobserved, I saw him board and row
The boat, and as unaided then, but slow

Toward the ship and reach her, saw him too,
His vessel board. What would from thence ensue
I could not guess. The absence of the twain
Who had accompanied him, he might explain
Perchance by injury or accident
Or death or from some unforseen event,
And if inclined might simulate concern
And make arrangements for their quick return;
Thus man the boat forthwith and have her go
(Upon a wild-goose-chase as he would know)
To find, and to the ship the injured bear
For more appropriate attention there.
But yet he might not bother to explain —
Indeed their curiosity disdain —
His very silence would his wish portend
And his harsh discipline their own commend.
But hawkeyed ever, he was bound to note
The absence port or starboard of the boat
And would on seeing neither boat nor me
Make, as I reasoned, due inquiry;
And of the consequence would search around
Until the boat then missing had been found.

'Twas as I guessed. There passed few minutes when
The boat, the Captain in her and two men
Shot from the vessel's starboard side and bore
Toward the South to search the further shore.
He did not think, nor dared to think that I

Was on the isle, that I was there to spy
And could bear witness to his infamy.
But when they'd searched the shore without success
They could, or as I thought, do nothing less
Than sail and search the nearer shores awhile
And then at last investigate the isle.

'Twas so, the boat was turned and Northward bore
Directly for the Kelly's Island shore
To search no doubt the isle, and I could see
That in the end they would discover me!
Aware of my grave peril, desp'rately
I sought out means for my delivery.
The boat came on and in a little while
Would touch the isle; but ere she reached the isle
She turned, or as it seemed, she spun around
And headed Southward, to our vessel bound,
As though, frustrated by a dreaded foe —
That foe, I was at once to know, for lo,
As I glanced East from there a frigate loomed
And I that instant knew our ship was doomed!
For she was helpless then, and unprepared
For that which Eastward suddenly appeared.

The ship was masterless her Captain where
He had no chance to reach his vessel, ere
The frigate favoured by a fresh'ning gale
With royals billowing so soon would sail

Upon the hapless ship, or she would be
Sufficient nigh to make inquiry —
To search and seize the ship if it turned out
She had no lawful business hereabout —
And thus the shot that warned her to abide
Until the frigate should her fate decide.

Just as the Captain climbed his vessel's side
I heard her guns as reckless she replied.
I heard the frigate's cannon boom again,
And saw our foremast felled by ball or chain.
The frigate's guns I heard again, again
Till fore and aft our vessel lay aflame.

Upon the isle advantaged by its height,
I watched till ended that unequal fight —
Until the vessel with her crew went down
All slain in action, save a few to drown
Within the waters of Conception Bay
Or to await in durance to the day
Of trial, thence until must strike the clock
The hour set for Execution Dock.

And ere that fateful day had closed, I told
My tale, intending nothing to with-hold
From my deliverers; but as compelled
The story of the packet, I with-held.

My tale though strange, supported by my youth
At length acceptance gained as simple truth;
And cross examination was I thought
For their persuasion less, than for their sport.

I asked the old man how he could so tell
Of ships and master and of what befell
The boy; so much about the buried gold —
As briefed complete for his reply, he told
Of how the boy was rescued carried home
To England, but in time inclined to roam
He'd followed Calvert to our Southern Shore
And died worn out of years at Baltimore.

Of how when death to him seemed imminent
He had himself prepared a document
Concerning all the years that he had spent
Aboard the ship as well as that event
Of his deliv'rance from the vessel vile;
Concerning too The Treasure of the isle,
The packet that he had received that day
The vessel sank within Conception Bay.

The document thus written further told
Of his suspicion of the hidden gold.
The packet had, the writing said, contained
A map; but this map had from use remained
By memories, the writer said, restrained.

And thus through withering years the map remained
Without suspicion of the worth it bore,
Until a blood descendant wont to pore
On ancient writings found and pondered o'er
The document, then dim and nigh obscure,
And came, relying on it to locate
The treasure and as finder of it, take.
But then the stranger doubtful of the mind
Of people here, decided he should find
Some one in whom he safely might confide,
Who'd be prepared to dig both deep and wide!

But who would dare, unless an outright knave
To meddle with or desecrate a grave
Along our shore — e'en though he were well paid —
But such an one the stranger might persuade
Upon production of the writing found
To dig with him into the middle mound!

He found his man but not till Autumn late
A man, at one with him confederate;
But found him not until November when
It seemed too late in view of weather then.

The stranger went; but came again in Spring
As by attraction of our sea to him,
For weather foul or weather fine sailed he
Along the shore or on the open sea;

And with his friend or in the boat alone
Would day by day about our waters roam.

We find a quality in Summer here
That is not found in summers known elsewhere;
But yet we hardly thought the love he bore
Toward the season or our friendly shore,
Was such, that he was satisfied to be
An idler only on our storied sea;
Or that he sought our lonesome isle to find
In isolation there, his peace of mind.
We hardly thought it would be worth his while
To spend his afternoons on Kelly's Isle
And there till ev'ning wait and idly lie
To witness then the sunset glorify
The rugged isle or until then abide
To view its golden path across the tide;
Nor did we think he'd idle in the sun
When that which he had come to do was done.
His ways were suspect from the first to last
And on his movements narrowed eyes were cast
Thus hardly strange was it to us that morn
To find, without a doubt, that he had gone.

No reason for his going might we note
Save from a clue discovered in the boat
He'd used for his excursions on the sea:
A coin or two of ancient mint which he

Regarded likely as sufficient for
Her hire whilst he sailed around our Shore.

And where might such rare coins as these be found
We asked of one another all around;
Although we felt no answer would be found
Till we ourselves had viewed the vacant mound.
As to the treasure's value no one knew;
But some of us our own conclusions drew,
For though the stranger went, 'twas noticed he
Who was his friend, knew rare prosperity.

(This is the story of our Treasure Isle;
And though you disbelieve it, or revile
The author for invention infantile,
It may for you some tedious hour beguile.)

Heber of Fair Haven

A few miles only from the broad speedway
Fair Haven drowses by Plancentia Bay,
Unmindful of or disinclined to care
About the pace men set themselves elsewhere.
Removed from vain endeavour aimless strife
Contented with their hardy way of life
They build their boats their wharves and stages here
Rebuild, renew or these again repair
To meet last year's or this year's wear and tear,
And fish from Spring till Autumn year by year
Upon their nets and varied gear to tend
Through weathers all for what the seas may send.

They're skillful boatmen doubtless, but seem slow
To understand the risk they undergo;
But though the seas be rough and rocks be nigh
They spot their moorings with unerring eye!
But it is clear today and from this hilltop, I
May far below the village homes descry
And trace the road that climbs and dips and bends
Until abrupt by Bob Crann's stage it ends.

Fair Haven southward looks upon the sea
Which seems today from all commotion free.
Southward from here a league or so away
Is Trinny Cove — from there on such a day
As this, you'll sometimes see the whales at play
Amongst the islands scattered through the Bay.

But staunch and stout that ship must be to bear
The winds that blow and seas that rise out there,
For old men hereabouts tell how they've seen
The stages go, and drift from Merasheen;
And we today note wreck the seas have thrown
Upon the strand and hither thither strewn.

The people of the village appear
To be united, and resemblance bear
To one large family, inclined to share
The fam'ly fortunes good or evil here.
Fair Haven does not change its dress to dine
Importance does not wear a dollar sign;
But if you're prone to yarn or apt to rhyme
The social ladder here you'll likely climb.

No one lives here, it seems, save fishermen
Their wives and fam'lies — and the Master, when
The school is open Autumn until Spring
Or early Summer, when the fish "strikes in"
For then the children join their elders here

And as a frolic in their labours share —
Then ancient men too frail to sail off land
Regain their pride, for they can lend a hand
And in some minor chores themselves engage,
And hear their prowess praised at their great age.

Here where the road drops nigh into the sea
Is Heber's Cot; but as for Heber he
Does little fishing; but in him we find
A man apart, of independent mind,
To argue prone, resourceful in debate,
A trifle given to exaggerate —
Can yarn of ventures over land and sea
Of love, romance of human tragedy,
And volunteer, should dubious you be,
The strictest proof of his veracity!
No one as Heber knows so much about
The habits of the salmon here and trout.
No one tries or thinks 'tis any use
To tell you more of caribou and moose;
And lean and lanky of a leisured stride,
In tangled woodlands he's a superb guide —
The rote that drifts in from Placentia Bay
Translates his route, an echo tells his way —

He does not fish so long as others here:
"Enough to eat and drink a rag to wear"
Is all he asks. The time he can't afford,

For life he finds is far too short to hoard.
Moreover treasures round about him wait
That only leisured eyes appreciate.
And though he be no "Jowler," few deny
His wisdom, or his age advice defy
In matters, not to do with fish or gear,
Yet of importance to the people here.
Not to the sea alone has he recourse —
Upon the land as well, he finds a source
Of sustenance:
In early August or in late July
Bakeapples as a golden largess lie,
Or yet as manna by kind heaven spread,
On marshes nigh that he is wont to tread
To glean therefrom; and other berries he
Will harvest as they ripen season'bly;
And many a spacious basket will he fill
From acres wild, he is not asked to till.

He has a mass of greying tousled hair,
For which he does not seem at all to care,
And pampers it with neither brush nor comb
But leaves its grooming to the winds alone.
His eyes of changeful colour blue or grey
Are thoughtful, calm and in some sort of way
They seem to "size you up" or weigh; but they
Occasionally are laughter-filled and gay.
His trousers never felt an ironing press

In short, he gives but scanty care to dress;
But then, nor do his neighbours here incline
To formal dress or lean to raiment fine.

And as I ponder Heber's fortunes, I
A truth refused or hidden, now descry
As from this clear cool stream I stoop to drink:
That riches are as we of riches think.

To Ray Riche, late of The Battery, St. John's, Fisherman

Now that he's gone, men who had known him say
The manner of his passing was the way
He would have wished, for he had loved the sea
Throughout his life and with rare constancy.

He was of stocky build and in the mould
Of one impassive to the storm and cold —
Of visage, aspect, not unlike the rock
So fashioned to contain and meet the shock
Of seas that rise from gales Northeasterly
Upon the bastions of his Battery.

Forthright was he and of convictions strong;
Not wont to quibble to compound a wrong.
Though bluff and hearty he was yet alert
To notice prejudice disposed to hurt
His fisher folk or threaten injury
To all who occupied themselves at sea.

He died at sea today —
For whilst out fishing from his little craft
A league or so off shore, his spirit passed —

'Tis but a sketch I offer of this man;
But you my friends, who knew him better than
Myself, with him more intimate, will meet
The requisites, his portrait to complete.

To a Sparrow in a Snow Storm

Here from my lofty window, I can view
The roof below, the chimney there, and through
The whirling drift can catch a glimpse of you
Perched purposeful close by the smoking flue
To find some comfort there, as I suppose,
Against the rigors of the frost and snows.

And by that token I have wondered oft
Why you refuse to wing your way aloft
And from the stifling snows, the ice and frost
Seek gentler climes where winds blow warm and soft;
Why you do not so poorly housed and fed
On alien leavings, a few crumbs of bread
Flung with the garbage, or occasion'ly
By your admirers or in charity,
Desert this place.

Oft have I watched you, as I thought, forlorn
Beside the chimney — your resource in storm —
And praised your grit throughout its violence;
Yet thought it wise that you would flee from hence

And leave this wind-swept place for good and all —
Or winter in some forest dense and tall.

Oh I have thought and think it passing strange
That you do not renounce the squalid range
The city slums, as pressed as you with care
And choose a kinder place, than this more fair.

I guess your strait; but after all suppose,
In fact assume — what others may propose
Concerns you not. You're like some folks I've seen
Who though their cottages be old and mean,
Abide no argument; but stubborn hold
Their patrim'ny beyond the grasp of gold:
For such no alien glory can atone
The loss of hut or hovel they call home.

If you by forest lore or legend know
About this place before men came, and how
Some forebear, though remote nursed here her brood
Your pref'rence may be better understood.

But who am I to argue thus with thee
For I myself might find felicity
On fabled isles, I've heard of; but forbear
Content as thou through weathers all to fare.

But you this morning offered no reproof
For my perplexity —
You were again upon the snow thatched roof,
In weather mild. The wind had ceased to blow
And you with comrades gambolled in the snow
Unruffled then and tranquil, and I knew
That life, without a doubt, seemed good to you:

I do not think you understand or know
Why you upon this battered roof bestow
Affection such or loyalty so great;
But as I muse on this, and calculate
Your constancy, your grit and valour there;
I can, as one who is not unaware
Of God in Nature, find within a sense
That is, or seems to be, of reverence.

Interlude

Mid August fair and warm, and on a day
That I remember well, for on the way
That I had chosen then, I glanced toward
A stone Cathedral and, by it, a board
Containing notices, wherefrom I read
That Evensong weekdays was daily said
At five —
The hour that the bell had just but tolled —
And on a sudden impulse, strode I through
The great arched doorway to an empty pew.

The Church was dim, the light thereto restrained,
By saints and angels on its windows stained.

Of middle height a lean ascetic man,
In vestments none, save cassock or sutan,
Of voice subdued but audible and clear
Recited canticle and collect prayer;
Read thoughtfully, not in a routine way,
The lessons, as appointed for the day.

In congregation there, I saw no more
Than two or three adults and half a score
Of teenaged children, and a tiny child,
Who had a doll, and who with it beguiled
The tedium of the worship there in play;
And wandered on her own unhindered way
About the Church;
And it is not unlikely too, that she
Upon her rambles found felicity,
As curious, she made discovery.
The little maiden no distinction made
Between the chancel and the nave, and strayed
About the great Cathedral here and there,
And where, but priest or acolyte might dare
Of sacrilege, irrev'rence unaware.
And so I think the good priest smiled
Upon the child.
Indeed, it seemed to me, he did not see
In her behaviour impropriety.
With her he might not reason remonstrate
And took the wisest course that he could take:
His Master, in such case, to imitate.

And as I watched the good priest there, I thought
Of Christ's displeasure when
His close and chosen followers opposed
The importuning parents who proposed
To have their little children touched by Him,

Whose virtues might preserve their sons from sin;
Of how the Master would not only touch
But took them in His arms, observing such
Were of the Kingdom and that all must be
To enter it, of their simplicity.
As for the elder children with her there,
No sweeter music did I ever hear
When they gave voice in chanticle and prayer.

The evensong was said; but I remained
To view the Gothic arches, windows stained,
The fluted columns chancel, altar, stalls
The lofty roof and massive masoned walls;
Then trode the spacious aisle, soft lit, not dim,
As all by contrast seemed, on entering,
With light that blazed without; but as I strode
Out through the fair Cathedral to the road
And mused on all the grace I saw within,
I sensed a worship there continuing
In all the beauty, artistry, it owned,
Or by its deathless artisans intoned!

To the Cathedral of
St. John the Baptist

As ancient Hebrews raised up altars where
They were persuaded of Jehovah's care
Your sires too, no less than they aware
Of grace divine, enshrined an altar here
And built and furnished of their own accord
Though scant their means, too scanty to afford
With lesser faith than theirs,
This Temple here —
So fashioned to withstand the wrath of storm
So wrought within His worship to adorn.

Rocklike it stands amidst the swirling tide
Of Commerce coursing by its ev'ry side;
Or as a citadel
Within whose massive masonry reside
A strength, a constancy,
Such as our Southside Hills to us confide.

All sorts of men conditions come in here

To worship, or because this House is fair,
Or yet stray in of purpose unaware,
Though conscious of its all inclusive air;
As to a Fold whose Shepherd still doth seek
To save unto the very last His sheep.
Within this hallowed place beyond the sound
Of raucous, restless traffic, peace is found
In meditation, prayer; and by no few
In study, contemplation as they view
The sculptured columns, arches, and aloof
The steep ascending haughty Gothic roof;
But even these, not wont to pray, confess
The beauty here of holiness.

But ah, what may we say without pretence
To language equal to the eloquence
Of things about you here that you may see;
Unless we be suspect of vanity;
For these do by their very presence own
A comeliness articulate of stone.

It is but gently lit, of rays restrained
By saints and angels on its windows stained,
And has a tranquil, chaste, consoling air
As of a holy presence near —
Of such a presence Israel aware
Could of the wilderness itself declare:
"This is none other but the House of God,"

And raise an altar on an alien sod!
A presence such, who trust His word may claim
Of places less than this, of lesser fame,
Where two or three are gathered in His name;
Some place obscure, as witness those with whom
He shared the Chalice in an upper room —

This House, you worship in, is doubtless fair
And for its grace alone, deserves your care;
But artistry and handiwork are vain,
No more than idols of a heathen fane
Effectual; unless these serve to bear
His holy presence unto you more near;
And may what excellence this House may own,
Illume your sev'ral ways to God alone.

Anonymity

His visage speech behaviour here became
A man of eminence although his name
Remained unknown; yet 'twas remarked that he
Had on the Feast of the Nativity
Come unannounced into the village here.

The stranger walked alone. The street was bare,
Were he to count but those who knew him there;
But season'bly on all he smiled, to find
Response from all as from a people kind
At one in charity; yet he could see
Unknown was he. Thus would he let it be,
Whilst he remained; but speculation ran
For years, within the village, since this man
Who seemed outlandish or from far away
Had walked upon their roadway Christmas Day.

Doubt lingered there; although it may be said
That this strange man then long presumed as dead
Had to his native village thus returned,
For he from year to year at Christmas yearned

For home and folks who kept the happy morn
As though the Holy Child had late been born;
That he'd returned, as drawn here from afar
His father's hearth and hamlet, his lode star.

The old man left the village just as he
In manner entered it, anonymously;
And for his largess spread there, made no claim,
Save that of honour to the Christ Child's name.
And if his own he chose not to confess,
He lit a legend there of selflessness
That had endured, and fragrant to this day,
Though generations since have passed away.

Anchorage

Change, change, change;
Unceasing and increasing change! — And we
Know indecision, doubt, perplexity
And drift and wander far beyond the range
Of voices olden, lured by others strange
From ancient precepts that our fathers knew
And tenets theirs immutable as true.

Ships all have need of ports or havens where,
They may take shelter and in calm repair
Storm damage and that harm from wear and tear,
They constant suffer, in their hulls and gear.

We too who voyage, and as it seems to me,
Upon a sea of change uncertainty
Resembling seas they sail upon, must know
Where we in strait may for our refuge go.

Albeit we for days may sail in peace
In weather fair and winds that cannot cease
To favour us, it seems; but cometh storm

Whereof, scarce conscious of it, we are borne
On unsuspected shoals and tossed about
(By arrogance, by indecision, doubt)
Until alarmed we ponder on retreat;
Yet search for haven to delay defeat;
But finding none, though search we howsoe'er,
We as reminded then of error, bear
For home
And anchorage
Upon an ancient faith,
One that unnumbered millions hath sufficed,
And peradventure doth today suffice
No few, who yet believe
In God
And in the saving power of His Christ.

The Issue

When I am troubled or perplexed of mind,
I look into some rev'rend tome to find
The answers there;
And though in travail of the soul 'tis meet,
That we should find some learned man discreet
And of his ghostly offices entreat,
I go occasion'lly, I must confess,
To those I understand in my distress.

I have a relish for the company
Of those who go in ships down to the sea —
Old sailormen —
Reliant on the firmament,
Intent
Upon the signs and tokens there to guide,
Of constant faith though voyage they e'er so wide.
Such men grow thoughtful, wise, without conceit
Through nightly watches on the lonely deep.

'Twas Christmas Day — the day

On which we celebrate the birth of Christ
Of the Messiah or the Promised One,
Though some insist that He is yet to come,
Recalling massacre and genocide
Reflecting as devouring mobs still ride
On those disposed to peace, and States divide,
Believing malice, hate and strife should cease
Were He, the Promised One, the Prince of Peace.

I think that I would know him at a glance
To be a seaman by his gait, his stance,
A seaman surely, though he might reside
A thousand miles from dock or waterside;
And such was he, for on a closer view
I found still more, that we each other knew.
I wondered then what he might have to say
Of men's misgivings or their doubts today;
And so acquaint, without undue delay,
I raised the issue
Left the case with him;
And he,
Without unseemly haste, had this to say:
He came to show the way
He had no doubt a purpose to fulfill
For man,
With no intent so e'er to do him ill
Or take from him the priv'lege of free will

His right to choose.

Not by an edict or decree
Intended He
To unify or to unite
Humanity
Compulsively.
There is no doubt He wished for peace; but still,
Not by restriant, enslavement of the will:
The son of God, Incarnate from above
No kingdom sought on Earth save that of Love
And thus it was, this Christ, Messiah, Lord
When one of His mistakenly had drawn
Was prompt to have him put aside the sword;
And yet again His wish divine revealed,
As He forthwith the wounded Malchus healed.

When he had finished speaking, I began
To view, to contemplate the plight of man,
Were he without freewill —
Were he to be denied the right to choose —
I scarce could think, for darkness seemed to fall
Upon me, as I sensed the loss of all
Were I to be denied the right to choose —
Or to decide how I my life might use,
In service here,
Withal in adoration prayer —
Demoted to the status of a slave,

To less —
A puppet strung to dance upon a grave,
Without a soul in heaven or earth to save!

The School Mistress

(To the memory of Sarah A. Somerton)

At seventeen, a comely maiden, bent
On learning; bookish, and intelligent —
At twenty, Mistress of a village school
With scanty pay, if absolute her rule,
Yet with emolument that they derive,
Who for the sole success of others strive —

At fifty, now a trifle more severe
Of countenance; in manner more austere —
Not from dislike but from her deep'ning care
For those, for whom she must for life prepare —

Retirement — She's now beyond fourscore,
A childless woman, lonely — No, not so,
For she hath children many, numb'ring more
Than she recalls, without some prompting now,
Who for her tutelage and constant care
Their Alma Mater lowly they revere
With no less reverence to theirs than they,
Who gratefully as well, their homage pay

To those of fame more fair,
And in their lustre share.

TODAY — we mark her passing or repose;
But note we not, nor can we now, the close
Of her accomplishments, or sum the gain
Assess the constant increase from the grain
She nourished in the brain;
For long and hard she wrought,
Unselfishly she taught;
And may the light she kindled here increase
And plead for her, O Lord, eternal peace.

On Wintering Abroad

I have no wish to pass the wintertime
In climes remote, though warmer then than mine,
Or to renounce my hearth and bolt my door,
If for one season only out of four;
For I have found no reason for alarm
In Winter, and have sensed as well his charm,
Benificence, as I the like in all
The others savour — Spring and Summer, Fall.

Let Winter have his fling, I say, and blow
And bluster, and his wholesome snow bestow
Upon the grateful earth,
And prove again to me and mine the worth
That we enjoy beside our flaming hearth.

As for myself, I take the Seasons four
As nature planned, and seek none to ignore
And notwithstanding weather foul, confess
No wish for boredom by a Winter less.

On Borrowed Time

'Tis strange that we who are disposed to pay
Physicians surgeons to prolong our day,
Are yet, despite the price of this delay,
At our wit's end to pass the time away.

As on our merchandise the prices soar,
As lesser grows our merchandise in store;
So we our lives assess, though deep they wane,
And precious weigh the moments that remain.

And we beyond the three score years and ten,
The span accepted by consent of men,
Who live henceforth, as we are apt to say,
On borrowed time, and scant, from day to day,
Do, notwithstanding this, oft-times neglect
To treat the moments lent us with respect,
And though so precious, or we say, yet choose
To pass in idleness or to misuse;
And older, older grow, as unaware,
Of duty, debt unto the borrowed year!

Time Out

I've heard it said or somewhere I have read,
That porters, hired lofty trails to tread,
At certain slopes or stages of their climb,
Or as decided by them time to time,
Will pause, though not of body-rest in need,
And wait, despite an urgency for speed
Until their souls, out-paced, catch up with them —
A purpose strange as thus expressed — but then,
Methinks there is in this more wisdom than
Is suspect by sophisticated man!

I met a man from distant parts who told,
Some lesson, as I reasoned, to unfold
For he was neither brash nor bold
Or talkative as some grown old;
But was of solemn measured speech,
Inclined to moralize or teach:
The story of two men who wished for fame,
And of the labours constant of the twain
Which I set down in brief,
Not with the license of a thief,

For whatsoever wisdom is
In this short tale, is his.

The sun goes down
One of the twain has known another day
Of triumph. He again has had his way;
But notwithstanding his complete success,
He fitful sleeps, affected by the stress
The like of which such men as he must bear,
Who to high office turn for their career.

The other man has felt as well the stress
Of his employment; but without success
And sleeps uneasily the night throughout
And wakes abruptly as disturbed by doubt,
To probe his conduct closely to detect
Some instance of omission or neglect
Upon his part, where-from to trace the blame;
But he discov'ring nothing to his shame,
Or to discredit him at last finds rest,
As one concerned with doing but his best.

But that was long ago,
When both of them were young
And they had but begun
Their promising careers.

One went from strength to strength till he became

A man preeminent, if blatant vain
Of his achievements; for 'twas constant plain
He wrought for little more than for his fame,
And that his love of public weal was less
Than that which he endeavoured to profess;
But this despite, he laboured long until
Of grievous ills (although against his will)
He quit his post, but as for him, too late
For of his inactivity frustrate
He lapsed into a state of mind insane
The victim doubtless of his lust for fame.

As for his vast achievements verily
His massive bust
Erected to preserve his memory
Has failed its trust
Reduced, as it hath been so long to dust.

The other whilst he was of body whole,
Reflected, paused, took counsel of his soul —
Thenceforth unchained pursued the cause
Of brotherhood and equal laws
Without concern for eulogy
Or masoned immortality.

One dies, and if he hath some claim to fame
The archives fail him, or misspell his name;
The other lives, for it is written he
Who selfless serves, survives eternally.

Ill fares the land

A goodly place, but most our people thought
The land was next to worthless when 'twas bought;
But he was landless then and wished to own,
As other men about him here, a home.
He got it for a trifling sum, but more
Than he could well afford, for he was poor.
'Twas rocky land; but stubbornly he cleared
His acres rude, and as we know he reared
Potatoes choice, and breast-high timothy.

The tools for clearing land, as I recall,
Were axe and crowbar, pick and sledge or mall;
And oft I've heard the racket as he swung
His sledge to split the rock that bound the drung.
I too have seen him as with calloused hand
He hacked the trash encumbering the land.
With such rude implements he toiled to clear
And render perch by perch his acres fair.

It lay some distance from the road, but won
An access to it by Delaney's drung

That bordered it, or hedged it by a row
Of trees that he had planted long ago.
The trees so grew and flourished that they flung
A sort of canopy upon the drung.
The place was small, but yet it could provide
A livelihood and let him put aside
A dollar now and then from his scant wage
Against mishaps or feebleness of age.

His cabin was a wondrous place, I thought,
And so, by his improvisation wrought:
Discarded things, a junkman would refuse,
He raised to honour by their altered use;
And what he bought, its purpose to revise,
The Vendor might no longer recognize.

The well, close by, rock-walled sufficient deep
To circumvent the dry midsummer's heat,
Was of such constancy, it satisfied
His neighbours' needs, when wells they owned had dried.
(But not for constant springs alone do we
Recall the well, for of its property
To cool, withal to hide; the well was where
He laid blueberry wine and choice spruce beer.)

But that was long ago —
Yet I who was so fond of it recall
The little farm, the peace upon it all —

Can almost sense the presence of its trees,
Or hear again the lisping of their leaves.

But that was long ago, I say
The old man withered, passed away
The farm that he had fashioned knew decline,
The era wore a larger dollar sign.
The cabin, fences, falling in decay
The farm, of boastful progress then the prey,
Was sold to those who planned — but in a diff'rent way,
From that of raising hay, to make it pay —
And thus it was the ale house that you see
Usurped the soil
Displaced the farmer's patient industry,
And so his lovely acres had become
Less than the wilderness whence these he won.

What change was here!
But change of course there's bound to be
And change itself hath constancy.
But you who knew his husbandry
Will bear with me,
Who now as you, his field no longer see,
Nor tossing crests of wind blown timothy.

To Signal Hill,
St. John's, Newfoundland

Men guess and speculate and deal in time,
To bind the infinite, or to divine
All origins, not I, but it must seem,
That thou art from creation and hast been
Since earth was fashioned, or convulsed to rear
Thy pillars narrowing the entrance here,
Into the harbour, delved, as of some plan,
Conceived in timelessness, designed for man
To hide from storm, to fit and to careen
His ships. What must thou in thy time have seen
If we may be permitted to confine
Or span thy presence by such means as time,
Since earth made first her cycle of the sun,
Or roused thee, of unrest within, as one
Of stature vested, fashioned to descry
The earth about, the ocean and the sky
As fractured lands fell in, yet seemed to rise
Or equipoise, remote, if in disguise;

As forests vanished leaving scarce a sign,
That men might mark, save in the pit and mine;
As force contrived, in cosmic order spent
The destiny of ev'ry element.

Yet out of all thy great antiquity,
I would, wert thou articulate, have thee,
Within the compass of our history,
Tell us the tale, as one, contempo'ry
With all the kings and captains of the cast,
That led the drama of this island's past;
And as the intimate of these, revive
Their ways and manners, as of men alive,
Remembered not as they, whom we contrive
To raise from parchment in some bleak archive!
Regroup Sir Humphrey's men upon King's Beach,
That we may savour well, plain seamen's speech,
And check the accents that methinks have clung
To ev'ry honest Port de Grave man's tongue;
Portray her company, resound the shout
As luffs the merchantman or comes about
Off Torbay Head, her cannons rammed to boom
The passage of the Narrows at high noon.
And with thy tale, I would have thee review,
The faults and foibles of the men you knew,
Who served the guns or slogged on sentry beat
And grouched of tongue, most likely indiscreet;
The songs they sang and verses they might quote,

From plays and sonnets Master Shakespeare wrote,
So late. 'Tis nigh two hundred years since when,
You felt the climb of Colonel Amherst's men
To meet the French — As of some interest —
Betwixt these brave, where did thy favours rest?
It matters not, for we thy slopes now claim,
And conquest means, at times, but better aim.
But on red war, I would that we should cease,
That we more fitly turn to arts of peace;
And as I seem to sense the strength of thee,
As one beyond the snare of flattery,
I would indeed, have thee confide to me,
As young Marconi flies his kites o'er thee,
And taps the signals of the century
Along two thousand miles of open sea,
Why, out of all the hills and mountains, he
Should choose to speak across the world from thee!

But I confess of ships, that as a boy
And grown man, I, vast leisure would employ
On their account, and often from thy crest,
I've viewed a thousand schooners, East and West,
In Summertime, within the harbour near
Along the waterfront, by dock and pier,
And in the stream, to take on salt and gear,
Or all-to-rights, to sail, if winds be fair,
At dawn, to fish along the Labrador,
The Belle Isle Straits, the Banks or Southern Shore.

And early March, as through the Narrows passed
The sealing ships, in pennant, yard and mast,
I'd count these all, the first unto the last,
Of wood and steel, into the hazard cast
Each Spring, and to their latest blast,
Or they would vanish in the icy vast;
Then turn about to look upon the town,
Upon the little houses, looking down,
Then out on bigger houses, as the street
Encounters others, widening to meet
The traffic there, and then, on those that greet
The thoroughfares by shops that must defeat
All reckoning, and then toward the hill,
Up to the great Cathedral, solemn, still
Inviting worshippers, or those, who may
Find solace there, or know a will to pray.

But, as your streamers March or April flew,
In their announcement of the ships that drew
Within thy view towards their homing port,
I would return, as one by habit taught,
And mount thy crest, to hail these from the hunt
As one, by one, they came from Gulf and Front.

O Mount, thy fame is sure, nor shall it cease
Until forgetfulness shall men release
From fealty; or honour shall have ceased
For thou dost hold the gateway at our East,

With access to domain, in boundary
Of half a continent by land and sea;
Yet mighty signal, raised above the sea,
I leave one word, the last of mine with thee,
As it hath been, still let thine office be
A beck'ning sign to all, who would be free!